REALLY EASY GUITAR

ROCK CLASSICS

22 SONGS WITH CHORDS, LYRICS & BASIC TAB

ISBN 978-1-5400-4078-7

Visit Hal Leonard Online at
www.halleonard.com

Contact us:
Hal Leonard
7777 West Bluemound Road
Milwaukee, WI 53213
Email: info@halleonard.com

In Europe, contact:
Hal Leonard Europe Limited
42 Wigmore Street
Marylebone, London, W1U 2RN
Email: info@halleonardeurope.com

In Australia, contact:
Hal Leonard Australia Pty. Ltd.
4 Lentara Court
Cheltenham, Victoria, 3192 Australia
Email: info@halleonard.com.au

GUITAR NOTATION LEGEND

Chord Diagrams

CHORD DIAGRAMS graphically represent the guitar fretboard to show correct chord fingerings.

- The letter above the diagram tells the name of the chord.
- The top, bold horizontal line represents the nut of the guitar. Each thin horizontal line represents a fret. Each vertical line represents a string; the low E string is on the far left and the high E string is on the far right.
- A dot shows where to put your fret-hand finger and the number at the bottom of the diagram tells which finger to use.
- The "O" above the string means play it open, while an "X" means don't play the string.

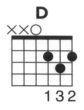

Tablature

TABLATURE graphically represents the guitar fingerboard. Each horizontal line represents a string, and each number represents a fret.

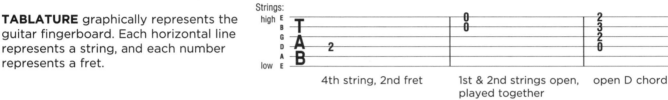

4th string, 2nd fret   1st & 2nd strings open, played together   open D chord

Definitions for Special Guitar Notation

HAMMER-ON: Strike the first (lower) note with one finger, then sound the higher note (on the same string) with another finger by fretting it without picking.

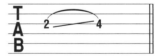

PULL-OFF: Place both fingers on the notes to be sounded. Strike the first note and without picking, pull the finger off to sound the second (lower) note.

LEGATO SLIDE: Strike the first note and then slide the same fret-hand finger up or down to the second note. The second note is not struck.

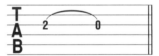

SHIFT SLIDE: Same as legato slide, except the second note is struck.

Additional Musical Definitions

N.C.
- No chord. Instrument is silent.

- Repeat measures between signs.

All Right Now

Words and Music by Andy Fraser and Paul Rodgers

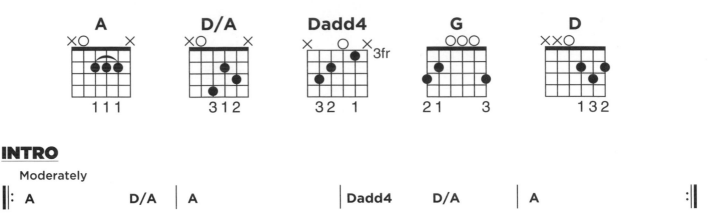

INTRO

Moderately

‖: A   D/A | A | Dadd4   D/A | A   :‖

VERSE 1

       A D/A A Dadd4   D/A   A   D/A A
There she stood in the street, smiling from her head to her feet. I said a, "Hey now, what is   this?

       Dadd4   D/A   A   D/A A
Now baby, maybe, maybe she's in need of a kiss." I said a, "Hey, what's your name, baby?

Dadd4   D/A   A   D/A A
Maybe we can see things the same. Now don't you wait or   hesitate.

       Dadd4   D/A   A
Let's move before they raise the parking rate."

CHORUS

A   G   D   A   G   D   A
All right now. Baby, it's all right now. All right now. Baby, it's all right now.

VERSE 2

       A D/A A Dadd4   D/A   A
I took her home to my   place, watching every move on her face. She said, "Look,

       D/A A   Dadd4   D/A   A   D/A A
what's your game, baby? Are you try'n' to put me in shame? I said a, "Slow, don't go so fast.

Dadd4   D/A   A   D/A A Dadd4   D/A   A
Don't you think that love can last?" She said, "Love? Lord above. Now you're try'n' to trick me in love."

REPEAT CHORUS

REPEAT VERSE 2

REPEAT CHORUS (REPEAT AND FADE)

Old Time Rock & Roll

Words and Music by George Jackson and Thomas E. Jones III

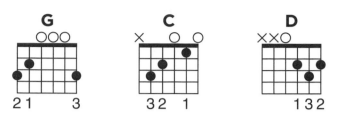

INTRO

Moderately

VERSE 1

                    G   C

Just take those old records off the shelf. I'll sit and listen to 'em by myself.

      D   G

Today's music ain't got the same soul. I like that old-time a rock and roll.

                                       C

Don't try to take me to a disco. You'll never even get me out on the floor.

      D   G

In ten minutes, I'll be late for the door. I like that old-time a rock and roll.

CHORUS

D   G   C

   Still like that old-time a rock and roll. That kind of music just soothes the soul.

                       D   G

I reminisce about the days of old with that old-time a rock and roll.

VERSE 2

                    G   C

Won't go to hear 'em play a tango. I'd rather hear some blues or funky old soul.

      D   G

There's only one sure way to get me to go: Start playing old-time a rock and roll.

                                     C

Call me a relic, call me what you will. Say I'm old-fashioned, say I'm over the hill.

      D   G

Today's music ain't got the same soul. I like that old-time a rock and roll.

REPEAT CHORUS (REPEAT AND FADE)

Baba O'Riley

Words and Music by Peter Townshend

(Capo 1st Fret)

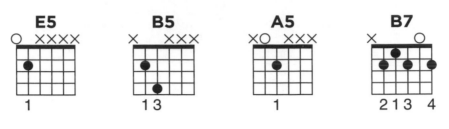

INTRO

Moderately

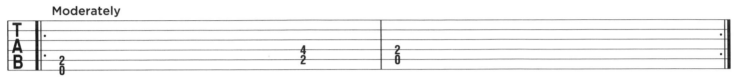

VERSE 1

E5   B5 A5   E5   B5 A5
Out here in the fields,   I fight for my meals.

E5   B5 A5   E5   B5   A5
I get my back into my livin'.

E5   B5 A5 E5   B5 A5
I don't need to fight   to prove I'm right.

E5 B5 A5   E5   B5   A5
I don't need to be forgiven, yeah, yeah, yeah, yeah, yeah.

INTERLUDE

Play 5 times

BRIDGE

B7
Don't cry, don't raise your eye. It's only teenage wasteland.

VERSE 2

```
E5            B5  A5   E5                    B5   A5
    Sally, take my hand.      We'll travel south 'cross land.

E5            B5   A5            E5           B5  A5
Put out the fire, and don't look past my shoulder.

E5            B5  A5   E5                    B5  A5
    The exodus is   here.      The happy ones are near.

E5           B5   A5                 E5      B5  A5
Let's get together before we get much older.
```

CHORUS

```
        E5         B5  A5          B5  E5       B5  A5
Teenage wasteland,           it's only teenage wasteland.

    B5  E5       B5  A5       B5  E5       B5  A5
Teenage wasteland, oh  yeah, teenage wasteland.
```

OUTRO

They're all

wast - ed!

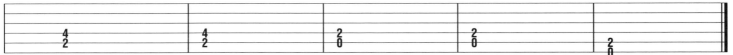

Born to Be Wild

Words and Music by Mars Bonfire

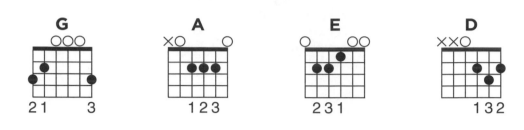

INTRO

Play 4 times

VERSE 1

Get your mo - tor run - nin',

head out on the highway.

Lookin' for adventure

and whatever comes our way.

PRE-CHORUS

G A E E G A E
Yeah, darlin' go make it happen, take the world in a love embrace.

G A E E G A E
Fire all of your guns at once and explode into space.

VERSE 2

w/ Verse Riff
I like smoke and lightning, heavy metal thunder, racin' with the wind, and the feelin' that I'm under.

REPEAT PRE-CHORUS

CHORUS

       E   G   A   G   E

Like a true nature's child, we were born, born to be wild. We can climb so high.   I never wanna die.

```
   E          D           E           D
‖: Born to be | wild.    |           |           :‖
```

REPEAT INTRO (2 TIMES)

REPEAT VERSE 1

REPEAT PRE-CHORUS

REPEAT CHORUS

REPEAT INTRO (REPEAT AND FADE)

Brown Eyed Girl

Words and Music by Van Morrison

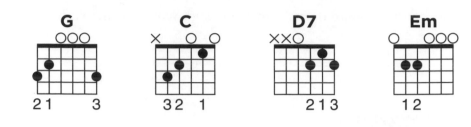

INTRO

Moderately fast

```
    0                     0
  0     0             3     1
0 2       2 0     1 3                0   2     0         2 0
                                                              4     4 0   2 4
```

VERSE 1

G   C   G   D7
Hey, where did we   go   days when the rains came?

G   C   G   D7
Down in the hollow,   playin' a new game.

G   C   G   D7
Laughin' and a runnin', hey, hey,   skippin' and a jumpin',

G   C   G   D7
in the misty morning fog with   our, our hearts a thumpin' and you,

C   D7   G   Em
               my brown-eyed girl.

C   D7   G   D7
You my   brown-eyed girl.

VERSE 2

G   C   G   D7
Now, what ever happened   to Tuesday and so slow?

G   C   G   D7
Goin' down the old mine with a   transistor radio.

G   C   G   D7
Standin' in the sunlight laughin',   hidin' 'hind a rainbow's wall.

G   C   G   D7
Slippin' and a slidin'   all along the waterfall with you,

C   D7   G   Em
               my brown-eyed girl.

C   D7   G   D7
You my   brown-eyed girl.   Do you remember when we used to sing?

CHORUS

G   C   G   D7
Sha, la, la, la, la, la, la, la, la, la, la, te, da.

G   C   G   D7
Sha, la, la, la, la, la, la, la, la, la, te, da.   La, te, da.

G | | N.C. | ‖

VERSE 3

G   C   G   D7
So hard to find my way   now that I'm all on my own.

G   C   G   D7
I saw you just the other day,   my, how you have grown.

G   C   G   D7
Cast my mem'ry back there, Lord.   Sometimes, I'm overcome thinkin' 'bout it.

G   C   G   D7
Makin' love in the green grass   behind the stadium with you,

C   D7   G   Em
       my brown-eyed girl.

C   D7   G   D7
You my   brown-eyed girl.   Do you remember when we used to sing?

OUTRO-CHORUS (REPEAT AND FADE)

G   C   G   D7
Sha, la, la, la, la, la, la, la, la, la, la, te, da.

Day Tripper

Words and Music by John Lennon and Paul McCartney

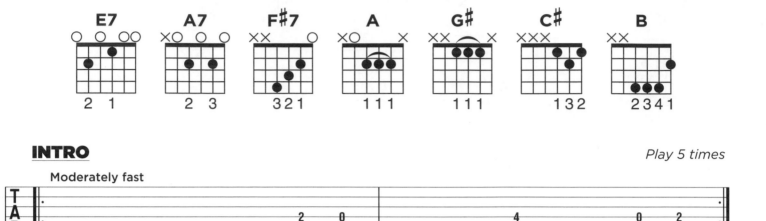

INTRO

Play 5 times

Moderately fast

```
T |--------------------------------|--------------------------------|
A |----------------2---0-----------|--------4-------2---0----2-------|
B |--0-------3---4---2--------------|------2--------------------------|
```

VERSE 1

E7   A7   E7
Got a good reason for taking the easy way out. Got a good reason for taking the easy way out, now.

CHORUS 1

      F#7   A G#   C#   B
She was a day tripper. One way ticket, yeah. It took me so long to find out,   and I found out.

REPEAT INTRO (2 TIMES)

VERSE 2

E7   A7
She's a big teaser. She took me half the way there. She's a big teaser.

E7
She took me half the way there, now.

CHORUS 2

      F#7   A G#   C#   B
She was a day tripper. One way ticket, yeah. It took me so long to find out,   and I found out.

REPEAT INTRO (2 TIMES)

VERSE 3

E7   A7

Tried to please her, she only played one-night stands. Tried to please her,

E7

she only played one-night stands, now.

CHORUS 2

F#7   A G#   C#   B

She was a day tripper. Sunday driver, yeah. It took me so long to find out,   and I found out.

REPEAT INTRO (4 TIMES)

OUTRO   REPEAT AND FADE

‖:   E7
    Day tripper, day tripper, yeah.   :‖

Don't Fear the Reaper

Words and Music by Donald Roeser

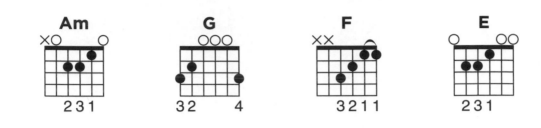

INTRO

Play 4 times

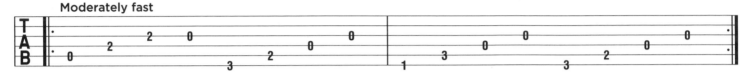

VERSE 1

Am G   F   G Am   G   F   G
All   our times have come.

Am G   F   G   Am G   F   G
Here   but now they're gone.

CHORUS 1

F   G   Am   F   E   Am   G   F
Seasons don't fear the reaper, nor do the wind, the sun or the rain. We can be like they are.

G   Am   G   F   G   Am   G   F   G
Come on, baby. Don't fear the reaper. Baby, take my hand. Don't fear the reaper. We'll be able to fly.

Am   G   F   G   Am   G   F   G
    Don't fear the reaper. Baby, I'm your man.

Am G   F G Am G   F   G   Am G   F G Am   G   F   G   Am
La,   la, la, la, la.   La,   la, la, la, la.

REPEAT INTRO (4 TIMES)

VERSE 2

Am G   F   G Am   G   F   G
Val - en - tine is done.

Am G   F   G   Am G   F   G
Here   but now they're gone.

CHORUS 2

F   G   Am   F   E   Am G F   G   Am   G
Romeo and Juliet are together in eternity.   Forty thousand men and women every day.

F   G   Am G F   G   Am   G   F
Forty thousand men and women every day.   Another forty thousand coming every day.

G   Am   G   F   G   Am   G   F   G
Come on, baby. Don't fear the reaper. Baby, take my hand. Don't fear the reaper. We'll be able to fly.

Am   G   F   G   Am   G   F   G
Don't fear the reaper. Baby, I'm your man.

Am G   F G Am G   F   G   Am G   F G Am   G   F   G   Am
La,   la, la, la, la.   La,   la, la, la, la.

REPEAT INTRO (4 TIMES)

VERSE 3

Am G   F   G Am   G   F   G
Love   of two is one.

Am G   F   G   Am   G   F   G
Here   but now they're gone.

CHORUS 3

F   G   Am   F   E   Am G   F   G
Came the last night of sadness, and it was clear she couldn't go on.   And the door was open, and

     Am   G   F   G   Am   G   F   G   Am
the wind appeared. The candles blew and then disappeared. The curtains flew and then he   appeared.

     G   F   G   Am   G   F G   Am   G F
Said don't be afraid. Come on, baby. And she had no fear.   And she ran to him.   They looked

G   Am   G F   G   Am G F G   Am   G   F   G
backward and said goodbye.   She had taken his hand.   Come on, baby. Don't fear the reaper.

OUTRO   REPEAT AND FADE

‖: Am   G | F   G   :‖

Fortunate Son

Words and Music by John Fogerty

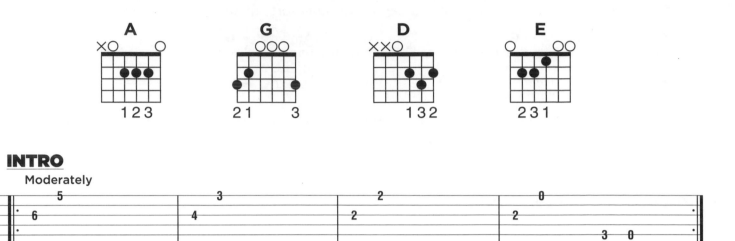

INTRO

Moderately

VERSE 1

A   G   D   A
Some folks are born, made to wave the flag,   ooh, their red, white and blue.

                          G   D   A
And when the band plays, "Hail to the Chief,"   ooh, they point the cannon at you.

CHORUS 1

A   E   D   A
But it ain't me,   it ain't me.   I ain't no senator's son, son.

              E   D   A
It ain't me,   it ain't me.   I ain't no fortunate one, no.

VERSE 2

A   G   D   A
Some folks are born, silver spoon in hand.   Lord, don't they help themselves, y'all?

                       G   D   A
But when the taxman come to the door,   Lord, the house look a like a rummage sale, yeah, now.

CHORUS 2

A   E   D   A
Well it ain't me,   it ain't me.   I ain't no millionaire's son, no, no.

              E   D   A
It ain't me,   it ain't me.   I ain't no fortunate one, no.

INTERLUDE

```
|--------------------------|--------------------------|--------------------------||--------------------------||
|--------------------------|--------------------------|--------------------------||--------------------------||
|--------------------------|--------------------------|----------------------3----||---------3--------5--------||
|.-8-----------------------|--7-----------------------|--7---/---4----------------||.--------4---/----6-------.||
|.-9-----------------------|--8-----------------------|--8---/--------------------||.-----------------------.-||
|--------------------------|--------------------------|--------------------------||--------------------------||
```

VERSE 3

A   G   D   A
Some folks inherit star-spangled eyes.   Ooh, they send you down to war, y'all.

                              G   D
And when you ask 'em, "How much should we give?"   Ooh, they only answer,

A
"More, more, more," y'all.

CHORUS 3

A   E   D   A
It ain't me,   it ain't me.   I ain't no military   son, son.

REPEAT AND FADE

‖: A   E   D   A
It ain't me, | it ain't me. | I ain't no fortunate | one, no.   :‖

Hey Joe

Words and Music by Billy Roberts

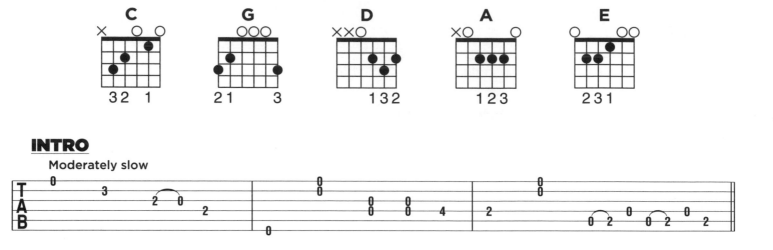

INTRO

Moderately slow

VERSE 1

C   G   D   A   E
Hey Joe,   uh, where you goin' with that gun in your hand?

C   G   D   A   E
Hey Joe,   I said where you goin' with that gun in your hand? Alright.

C   G   D   A   E
I'm goin' down to shoot my old lady,   you know I caught her messin' 'round with another man.

C   G   D   A   E
I'm goin' down to shoot my old lady,   you know I caught her messin' 'round with another man.

And that ain't too cool.

VERSE 2

C   G   D   A   E
Uh, hey Joe,   I heard you shot your woman down, you shot her down now.

C   G   D   A   E
Uh, hey Joe,   I heard you shot your old lady down, you shot her down in the ground.

C   G   D   A   E
Yes I did, I shot her.   You know I caught her messin' 'round, messin' 'round town.

C   G   D   A   E
Uh, yes I did, I shot her.   You know I caught my old lady messin' 'round town.

And I gave her the gun. I shot her.

VERSE 3

```
C       G  D  A                       E
Hey Joe,        uh, where you gonna run to now?

C       G      D  A                   E
Hey Joe, I said,        where you gonna run to now, where you, where you gonna go?

C               G           D  A           E
I'm goin' way down south,        way down to Mexico way.

C               G           D  A               E
I'm goin' way down south,        way down where I can be free.
```

OUTRO (FADE OUT)

```
C           G               D           A               E
Ain't no hangman gonna,     he ain't gonna put a rope around me.
```

You better believe it right now. I gotta go now.

```
C       G   D       A           E
Hey Joe,    you better run on down.    Goodbye everybody.
```

(I Can't Get No) Satisfaction

Words and Music by Mick Jagger and Keith Richards

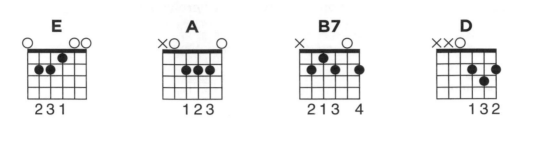

INTRO

Play 4 times

Moderately fast

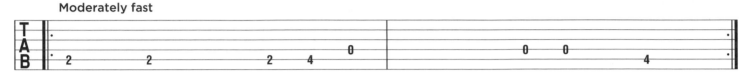

CHORUS 1

E   A   E   A
I can't get no   satisfaction.   I can't get no   satisfaction, 'cause I try

E   B7   E   A   E   D   E   D
and I try   and I try   and I try.   I can't get no,   I can't get no,

VERSE 1

E   D   E   D   E
When I'm drivin' in my car   and the man come on the radio; he's tellin' me more and more

D   E   D   E   D   E
about some useless information supposed to fire my imagination. I can't get no.

D   E N.C.   E   D   E   D
Oh, no, no, no.   Hey, hey, hey.   That's what I say.

REPEAT CHORUS 1

VERSE 2

E   D   E   D   E
When I'm watchin' my TV   and a man comes on and tells me how white my shirts can be.

D   E   D   E   D   E
But he can't be a man 'cause he doesn't smoke the same cigarettes as me.   I can't get no.

D   E N.C.   E   D   E   D
Oh, no, no, no.   Hey, hey, hey.   That's what I say.

CHORUS 2

E		A		E		A
I can't get no		satisfaction.		I can't get no		girl reaction, 'cause I try

E		B7		E		A		E		D		E		D
and I try		and I try		and I try.		I can't get no,		I can't get no,			

VERSE 3

E		D		E		D
When I'm ridin' 'round the world,		and I'm doin' this, and I'm signin' that; and I'm			

E		D		E		D
tryin' to make some girl,		who tells me, "Baby, better come back maybe next week. 'Cause you			

E		D		E	D	E N.C.		E	D	E	D
see I'm on a losing streak." I can't get no.		Oh, no, no, no.		Hey, hey, hey.		That's what I say.					

OUTRO (FADE OUT)

E	D	E	D	E	D	E	D	E
I can't get no.	I can't get no.	I can't get no	satisfaction,	no satisfaction,				

D	E	D	E	D	E	D
no satisfaction,	no satisfaction.	I can't get no…				

Iron Man

Words and Music by Frank Iommi, John Osbourne, William Ward and Terence Butler

INTRO

Slow

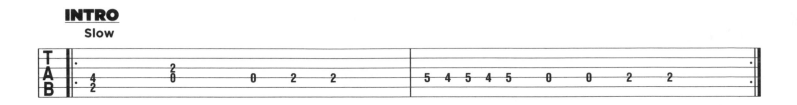

VERSE 1

w/ Intro Riff

Has he lost his mind? Can he see or is he blind?

Can he walk at all, or if he moves will he fall?

REPEAT INTRO (1 TIME)

VERSE 2

w/ Intro Riff

Is he live or dead? I see thoughts within his head.

We'll just pass him there. Why should we even care?

INTERLUDE

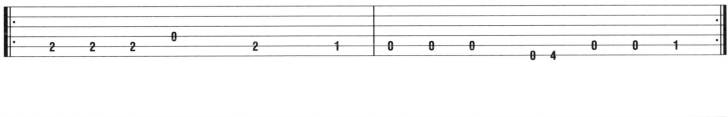

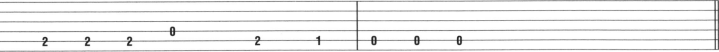

REPEAT INTRO (2 TIMES)

VERSE 3

w/ Intro Riff
He was turned to steel in the great magnetic field,

when he travelled time for the future of mankind.

BRIDGE 1

Nobody wants him,   he just stares at the world.

```
|-------------------|---------------|-------------------234-|-------------------234-|
|-------------------|-2-------------|------------02-234-----|------------02-234-----|
|-2-----------------|-0-------------|-2--2--2---------------|-2--2--2---------------|
|-0-----------------|---------------|-----------------------|-----------------------|
|-------------------|---------------|-----------------------|-----------------------|
|-------------------|---------------|-----------------------|-----------------------|
```

Planning his vengeance   that he will soon unfurl.

REPEAT INTRO (2 TIMES)

VERSE 4

w/ Intro Riff
Now the time is here for Iron Man to spread fear.

Vengeance from the grave kills the people he once saved.

BRIDGE 2

w/ Bridge 1 riff
Nobody wants him,   they just turn their heads.

Nobody helps him.   Now he has his revenge.

REPEAT INTRO (2 TIMES)

VERSE 5

w/ Intro Riff
Heavy boots of lead, fills his victims full of dread.

Running as fast as they can, Iron Man lives again!

REPEAT INTERLUDE

Life in the Fast Lane

Words and Music by Don Henley, Glenn Frey and Joe Walsh

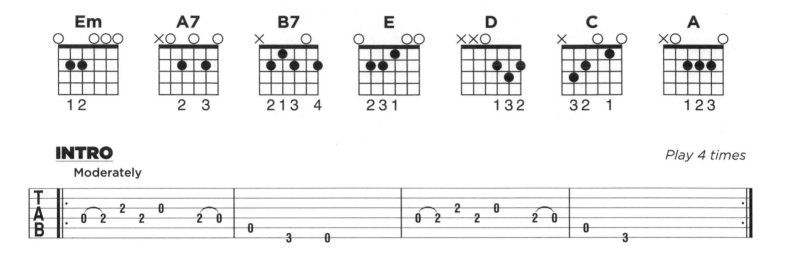

INTRO

Moderately

Play 4 times

VERSE 1

Em
He was a hard-headed man. He was brutally handsome and she was terminally pretty.

She held him up, and he held her for ransom in the heart of the cold, cold city. He had a

A7　　　　　　　　　　　　　　　　　**Em**
nasty reputation as a cruel dude. They said he was ruthless. They said he was crude. They had

B7　　　　　　　　　　　　　　　　　　　　　**A7**
one thing in common, they were good in bed. She'd say,　 "Faster, faster, the lights are turnin' red."

CHORUS

Em
　Life in the fast lane. Surely make you lose your mind. Life in the fast lane. Yeah.

VERSE 2

Em
Eager for action and hot for the game. The coming attraction, the drop of a name. They knew

all the right people. They took all the right pills. They threw outrageous parties. They paid

　　　　　　　　　　　　A7　　　　　　　　　　　　　　　**Em**
heavenly bills. There were　 lines on the mirror, lines on her face. She pretended not to notice,

　　　　　　　　B7　　　　　　　　　　　　　　　　　　**A7**
she was caught up in the race. Out every evening until it was light. He was too tired to make it.

She was too tired to fight about it.

CHORUS 2

Em
Life in the fast lane. Surely make you lose your mind. Life in the fast lane. Yeah.

Life in the fast lane. Everything, all the time. Life in the fast lane. Uh, huh.

VERSE 3

Em
Blowin' and burnin', blinded by thirst. They didn't see the stop sign, took a turn for the worse.

She said, "Listen, baby. You can hear the engine ring. We've been up and down this highway,

                                              A7
haven't seen a goddamn thing." He said,   "Call the doctor. I think I'm gonna crash."

      Em   **B7**
"The doctor say he's comin', but you gotta pay him in cash." They went rushin' down that freeway.

                             A7
Messed around and got lost.   They didn't care, they were just dyin' to get off and it was...

REPEAT CHORUS 2

INTERLUDE

E
    Life in the fast | lane.   **D** | | |
C
    Life in the fast | lane.   **A** | | ‖

OUTRO   *REPEAT AND FADE*

‖: **Em** | :‖

Refugee

Words and Music by Tom Petty and Mike Campbell

(Capo 2nd Fret)

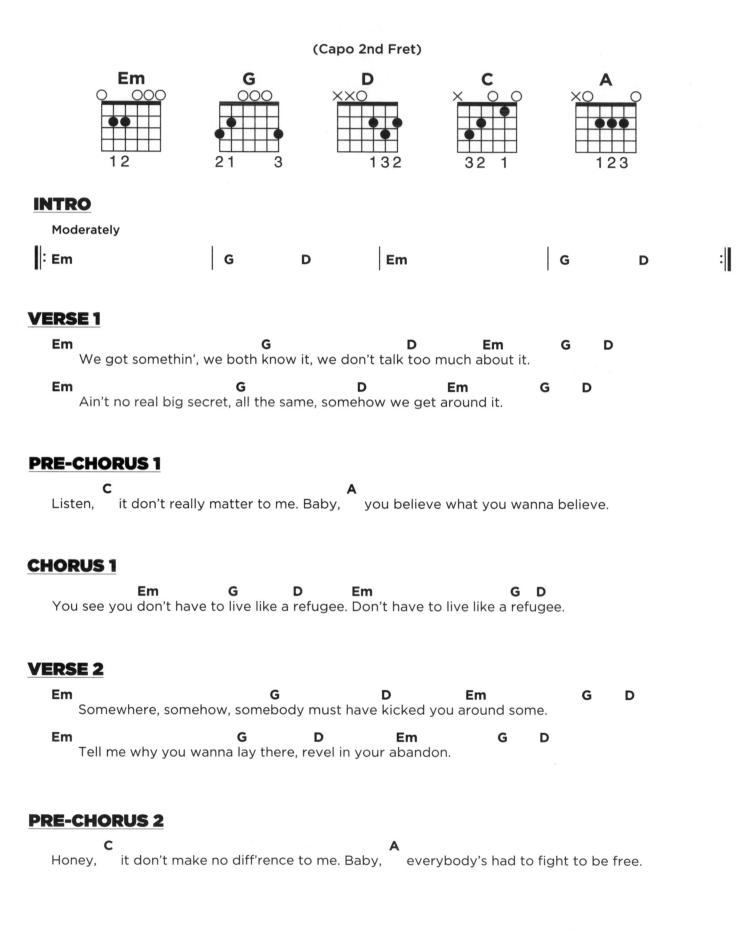

INTRO

Moderately

‖: Em | G   D | Em | G   D :‖

VERSE 1

Em   G   D   Em   G   D
    We got somethin', we both know it, we don't talk too much about it.

Em   G   D   Em   G   D
    Ain't no real big secret, all the same, somehow we get around it.

PRE-CHORUS 1

    C   A
Listen,   it don't really matter to me. Baby,   you believe what you wanna believe.

CHORUS 1

    Em   G   D   Em   G D
You see you don't have to live like a refugee. Don't have to live like a refugee.

VERSE 2

Em   G   D   Em   G   D
    Somewhere, somehow, somebody must have kicked you around some.

Em   G   D   Em   G   D
    Tell me why you wanna lay there, revel in your abandon.

PRE-CHORUS 2

    C   A
Honey,   it don't make no diff'rence to me. Baby,   everybody's had to fight to be free.

CHORUS 2

Em   G   D   Em   G D
You see you don't have to live like a refugee. Don't have to live like a refugee.

Em   G   D   Em   G D
Now baby, you don't have to live like a refugee. Don't have to live like a refugee.

BRIDGE

D   G
Baby, we ain't the first.   I'm sure a lot of other lovers been burned.

C   D
Right now this seems real to you, but it's one of those things you got to feel to be true.

VERSE 3

Em   G   D   Em   G   D
Somewhere, somehow, somebody must have kicked you around some.

Em   G   D   Em   G   D
Who knows? Maybe you were kidnapped, tied up, taken away and held for ransom.

PRE-CHORUS 3

C   A
Honey,   it don't really matter to me. Baby,   everybody's had to fight to be free.

CHORUS 3

Em   G   D   Em   G D
You see you don't have to live like a refugee. Don't have to live like a refugee.

Em   G   D   Em   G D
No you don't have to live like a refugee. Don't have to live like a refugee.

Em   G   D   Em   G D
Baby, you don't have to live like a refugee. Don't have to live like a refugee.

REPEAT INTRO (REPEAT AND FADE)

Rock and Roll All Nite

Words and Music by Paul Stanley and Gene Simmons

(Capo 1st Fret)

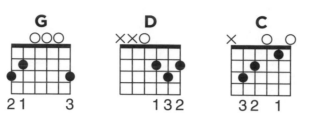

INTRO

Moderately fast

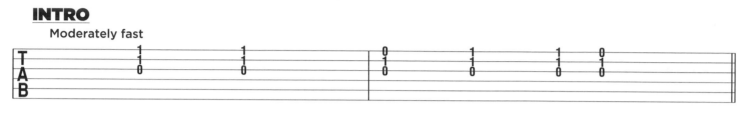

```
|: G          | D          :|
```

VERSE 1

G   D   G   D
You show us everything you've got.   You keep on dancin', and the room gets hot.

C   D   w/ Intro Riff
You drive us wild. We'll drive you crazy.

G   D   G   D
And you say you wanna go for a spin.   The party's just begun. We'll let you in.

C   D   w/ Intro Riff
You drive us wild. We'll drive you crazy.

PRE-CHORUS

You keep on shout - in', you   keep on shout - in',

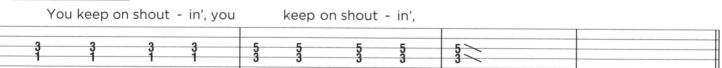

CHORUS

G   C D   G   C D
I wanna rock and roll all nite   and party every day. I wanna rock and roll all nite   and party every day.

G   N.C.
I wanna rock and roll all nite and party every day. I wanna rock and roll all nite and party every day.

REPEAT INTRO

VERSE 2

G   D   G   D
You keep on sayin' you'll be mine for a while.   You're lookin' fancy, and I like your style.

C   D   **w/ Intro Riff**
You drive us wild. We'll drive you crazy.

G   D   G   D
You show us everything you've got.   Baby, baby, that's quite a lot.

C   D   **w/ Intro Riff**
And you drive us wild. We'll drive you crazy.

REPEAT PRE-CHORUS

REPEAT CHORUS

REPEAT INTRO

OUTRO

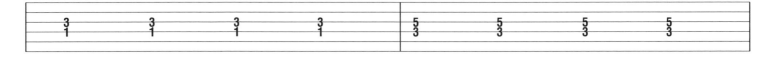

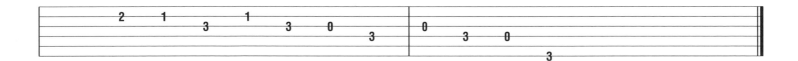

Smoke on the Water

Words and Music by Ritchie Blackmore, Ian Gillan, Roger Glover,
John Lord and Ian Paice

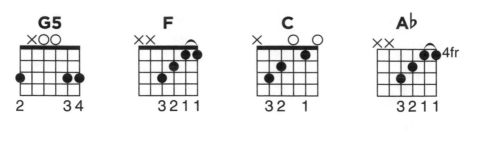

INTRO

Play 6 times

Moderately

```
T  ┌╥─────────────────┬─────────────────┬─────────────────┬─────────────────╥┐
A  │║ 0  3  5    0     │ 3  6  5    0    │ 0  3  5    3    │ 0              ║│
B  │║ 0  3  5    0     │ 3  6  5    0    │ 0  3  5    3    │ 0              ║│
   └╨─────────────────┴─────────────────┴─────────────────┴─────────────────╨┘
```

VERSE 1

   G5   F   G5
We all came out to Montreaux on the Lake Geneva shoreline

                       F   G5
to make records with the mobile,   we didn't have much time.

                               F   G5
But Frank Zappa and the Mothers were at the best place around.

                             F   G5
But some stupid with a flare gun burned the place to the ground.

CHORUS

   C   Ab   G5   C   Ab
Smoke on the water,   a fire in the sky. Smoke on the water.

REPEAT INTRO (2 TIMES)

VERSE 2

G5   F   G5
     They burned down the gamblin' house. It died with an awful sound.

                             F   G5
A Funky Claude was running in and out,   pulling kids out the ground.

                         F   G5
When it all was over, we had to find another place.

                             F   G5
But Swiss time was running out. It seemed we would lose the race.

CHORUS

```
C               Ab   G5              C           Ab
Smoke on the water,    a fire in the sky. Smoke on the water.
```

REPEAT INTRO (2 TIMES)

VERSE 3

```
G5                                        F      G5
    We ended up at the Grand Hotel. It was empty, cold and bare.

                                            F           G5
But with the Rolling truck Stones thing just outside,    making our music there.

                                        F      G5
With a few red lights, a few old beds, we made a place to sweat.

                                      F        G5
No matter what we get out of this, I know,    I know we'll never forget.
```

CHORUS

```
C               Ab   G5              C           Ab
Smoke on the water,    a fire in the sky. Smoke on the water.
```

REPEAT INTRO (REPEAT AND FADE)

Sunshine of Your Love

Words and Music by Jack Bruce, Pete Brown and Eric Clapton

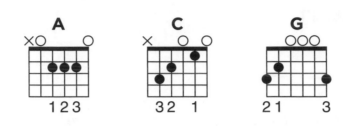

Play 4 times

INTRO

Moderately

VERSE 1

w/ Intro Riff
It's getting near dawn

when lights close their tired eyes.

I'll soon be with you, my love,

to give you my dawn surprise. I'll

be   with   you,   dar - ling,   soon.

I'll be with you when the stars start falling.

REPEAT INTRO (2 TIMES)

CHORUS

A N.C.   C   G   A N.C.   C   G
I've been wait - ing so   long   to be where   I'm go - ing

A N.C.   C   G   A
in the sun - shine of   your love.

REPEAT INTRO (1 TIME)

VERSE 2

w/ Intro Riff
I'm with you, my love,

the light shining through on you.

Yes I'm with you, my love.

It's the morning and just we two. I'll

stay   with   you,   dar   -   ling,   now.

```
|------------------------------------|-------------------------------------|
|------------------------------------|-------------------------------------|
|------------------------------------|--------------3----------------------|
|--5----5----3----5------------------|--------5---------------5------------|
|--------------------------5------4--|----3--------------------------------|
|------------------------------------|-------------------------------------|
```

I'll stay with you till my seeds are dried up.

REPEAT INTRO (2 TIMES)

REPEAT CHORUS

REPEAT INTRO (2 TIMES)

REPEAT VERSE 2

REPEAT INTRO (2 TIMES)

OUTRO-CHORUS

A N.C.   C G A N.C.   C G
I've been wait - ing so   long,   I've been wait - ing so   long,

A N.C.   C G A N.C.   C   G
I've been wait - ing so   long   to be where   I'm go - ing

A N.C. C G A
in the sun - shine of   your love.

Sweet Home Alabama

Words and Music by Ronnie Van Zant, Ed King and Gary Rossington

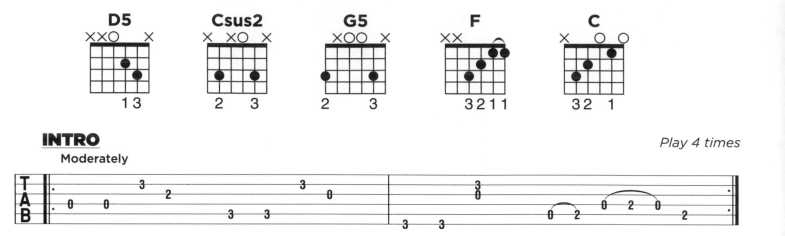

INTRO

Moderately

Play 4 times

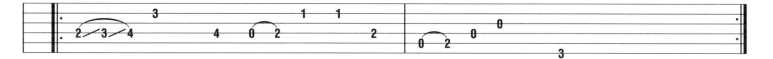

VERSE 1

D5　　Csus2　　　　G5　　D5　　　　Csus2　　　　G5
Big wheels keep on turnin',　　carry me home to see my kin.

D5　　　　Csus2　　　　　G5　　　D5　　　　Csus2　　　G5
Singin' songs about the southland.　　I miss Alabamy once again, and I think it's a sin.

INTERLUDE

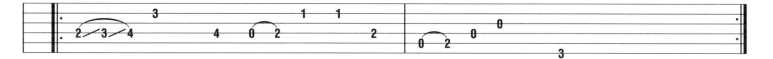

VERSE 2

D5　　　　　　　Csus2　　　G5　　D5　　　　　Csus2　　　G5
Well, I heard Mister Young sing about her.　　Well, I heard old Neil put 'er down.

D5　　　　　　Csus2　　　G5　　D5　　　Csus2　　　　　　G5
Well, I hope Neil Young will remember,　　a southern man don't need him around, anyhow.

CHORUS

D5　　Csus2　G5　D5　　　　Csus2　　　G5
Sweet home Alabama,　　where the skies are so blue.

D5　　Csus2　G5　D5　　　Csus2　　　　G5
Sweet home Alabama,　　Lord, I'm comin' home to you.

VERSE 3

D5   Csus2   G5   F C D5   Csus2   G5
In Birmingham, they love the gov'nor, boo, boo, hoo. Now we all did what we could do.

D5   Csus2   G5   D5   Csus2   G5
Now Watergate does not bother me,   does your conscience bother you? Tell the truth.

REPEAT CHORUS

REPEAT INTERLUDE (2 TIMES)

VERSE 4

D5   Csus2   G5   D5   Csus2   G5
Now Muscle Shoals has got the Swampers,   and they been known to pick a song or two.

D5   Csus2   G5   D5   Csus2   G5
Lord, they get me off so much.   They pick me up when I'm feelin' blue, and now how 'bout you?

REPEAT CHORUS (2 TIMES)

OUTRO   *REPEAT AND FADE*

‖: D5   Csus2 | G5   :‖

Whole Lotta Love

Words and Music by Jimmy Page, Robert Plant, John Paul Jones,
John Bonham and Willie Dixon

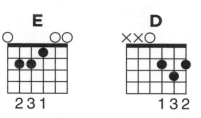

INTRO
Moderately

Play 4 times

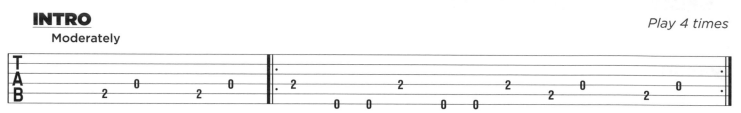

VERSE 1

w/ Intro Riff
You need coolin', baby, I'm not foolin'.

I'm gonna send you back to schoolin'.

Way down inside, honey, you need it.

I'm gonna give you my love. I'm gonna give you my love.

CHORUS

E	D	E	D	E

Wanna whole lotta love.   Wanna whole lotta love.

D	E	D	w/ Intro Riff

Wanna whole lotta love.   Wanna whole lotta love.

VERSE 2

w/ Intro Riff
You've been learnin', and baby, I been learnin'.

All them good times, baby, baby, I've been yearnin'.

Way, way down inside, honey, you need.

I'm gonna give you my love. I'm gonna give you my love.

REPEAT CHORUS

VERSE 3

w/ Intro Riff
You've been coolin', and baby, I've been droolin'.

All the good times, baby, I've been misusin'.

Way, way down inside, I'm gonna give you my love.

I'm gonna give you every inch of my love. I'm gonna give you my love.

Hey, alright, let's go!

REPEAT CHORUS

REPEAT INTRO (REPEAT AND FADE)

Wish You Were Here

Words and Music by Roger Waters and David Gilmour

VERSE 1

  C   D   Am   G
So, so you think you can tell heaven from hell, blue skies from pain.

               D   C   Am   G
Can you tell a green field from a cold steel rail, a smile from a veil? Do you think you can tell?

            C   D   Am   G
Did they get you to trade your heroes for ghosts, hot ashes for trees, hot air for a cool breeze,

            D   C   Am   G
cold comfort for change? Did you exchange a walk-on part in the war for a lead role in a cage?

REPEAT INTRO

VERSE 2

C   D
    How I wish, how I wish you were here. We're just

Am   G
two lost souls swimming in a fishbowl,   year after year.

D   C
    Running over the same old ground,   what have we found?

          Am   G
The same old fears, wish you were here.

REPEAT INTRO (REPEAT AND FADE)

You Really Got Me

Words and Music by Ray Davies

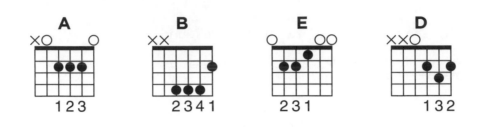

INTRO

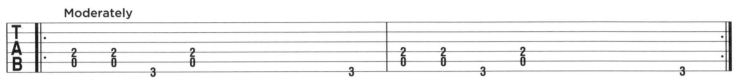

VERSE 1

A
Girl, you really got me goin', you got me so I don't know what I'm doin' now.

Yeah, you really got me now, you got me so I can't sleep at night.

B
Yeah, you really got me now, you got me so I don't know what I'm doin', ah. Oh,

E
yeah, you really got me now, you got me so I can't sleep at night. You really got me.

You really got me. You really got me.

INTERLUDE

D

VERSE 2

A
See, don't ever set me free, I always wanna be by your side.

Girl, you really got me now, you got me so I can't sleep at night.

B
Yeah, you really got me now, you got me so I don't know what I'm doin', ah. Oh,

E
yeah, you really got me now, you got me so I can't sleep at night. You really got me.

You really got me. You really got me.

INTERLUDE

D

REPEAT INTRO

REPEAT VERSE 2

OUTRO

```
|--0--------0--------0--------|--0--------------------||
|--0--------0--------0--------|--0--------------------||
|--1--------1--------1--------|--1--------------------||
|--2--------2--------2--------|--2--------------------||
|--2--------2--------2--------|--2--------------------||
|--0--------0--------0--------|--0--------------------||
```

You Shook Me All Night Long

Words and Music by Angus Young, Malcom Young and Brian Johnson

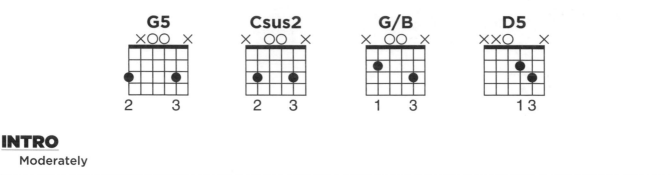

INTRO
Moderately

```
  .|0                    5      5 0   5 0 7  |               |0        0  0 7 0 7 7 |.
  .|0                    5      5 0   5 0 7  |               |0        0  0 7 0 7 7 |.
```

VERSE 1

w/ Intro Riff

She was a fast machine, she kept her motor clean. She was the best damn woman that I ever seen.

She had the sightless eyes, tellin' me no lies, knockin' me out with those American thighs. Takin'

more than her share, had me fightin' for air. She told me to come, but I was already there. Cuz the

```
walls    start    shak - in',    the    earth   was    quak - in',   my  mind

     0                              5      5   0      5        0  7
     0                              5      5   0      5        0  7
```

```
        was  ach  -  in',     and   we   were    mak  -  in'  it.  And

  7    7    7    7    7    7    7    7    7  | 7   7    7    7    7    7    7    7  |
  7    7    7    7    7    7    7    7    7  | 7   7    7    7    7    7    7    7  |
```

CHORUS

```
G5          Csus2  G/B    D5      Csus2       G/B
you shook me all        night    long.
```

```
      G5            Csus2  G/B    D5      Csus2       G/B
Yeah, you shook me all        night    long.
```

VERSE 2

w/ Intro Riff

Workin' double-time on the seduction line, she was one of a kind. She's just mine, all mine.

Wanted no applause, just another course. Made a meal out of me and came back for more.

Had to cool me down to take another round, now I'm back in the ring to take another swing. Cuz the

```
         walls      was      shak - in',      the     earth      was      quak - in',  my   mind
|-----------------------------------------|-----------------------------------------------------|
|-----------------------------------------|-----------------------------------------------------|
|------------------------------5----------|----5------0-----------5----------0-------7-----------|
|------0-----------------------5----------|----5------0-----------5----------0-------7-----------|
|------0----------------------------------|-----------------------------------------------------|
|-----------------------------------------|-----------------------------------------------------|
```

```
         was     ach -  in',      and     we    were     mak -  in'  it.  And
|-------------------------------------------|-----------------------------------------------------|
|-------------------------------------------|-----------------------------------------------------|
|--7----7----7----7----7----7----7----7-----|--7----7----7----7----7----7----7----7---------------|
|--7----7----7----7----7----7----7----7-----|--7----7----7----7----7----7----7----7---------------|
|-------------------------------------------|-----------------------------------------------------|
|-------------------------------------------|-----------------------------------------------------|
```

OUTRO-CHORUS

G5	Csus2	G/B	D5	Csus2	G/B

you shook me all   night   long.   Ah,

G5	Csus2	G/B	D5	Csus2	G/B

you shook me all   night   long.   Yeah, yeah,

G5	Csus2	G/B	D5	Csus2	G/B

you shook me all   night   long.   You really got me, and

G5	Csus2	G/B	D5	Csus2	G/B

you shook me all   night   long.   Yeah, you shook me,

D5	Csus2	G/B

   yeah, you shook me

```
                         all          night          long.
|-----------------------------|-----------------------------|-----------------------------|--|
|-----------------------------|-----------------------------|-----------------------------|--|
|--7--7--7--7--7--7--7--7------|--7--7--7--7--7--7--7--7------|--7--7--7--7--7--7--7--7------|--|
|--7--7--7--7--7--7--7--7------|--7--7--7--7--7--7--7--7------|--7--7--7--7--7--7--7--7------|--|
|-----------------------------|-----------------------------|-----------------------------|--|
|-----------------------------|-----------------------------|-----------------------------|--|
```

Ramblin' Man

Words and Music by Dickey Betts

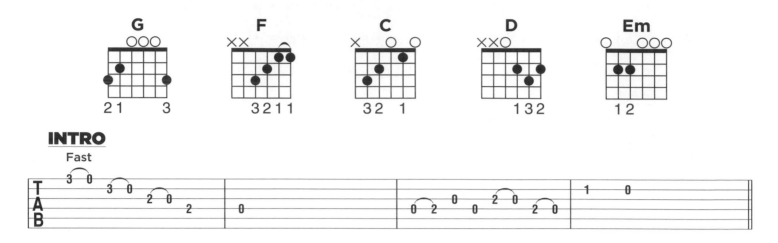

INTRO

Fast

CHORUS

| G | F | C | G | | | C | | D |

Lord, I was born a ramblin' man. Try'n' to make a living and doin' the best I can.

| C | | G | Em | | C | G | D | | G |

And when it's time for leavin' I hope you'll understand   that I was born a ramblin' man.

VERSE 1

| G | C | G | | | C | | D |

Well, my father was a gambler down in Georgia, and he wound up on the wrong end of a gun.

| C | G | Em | | C | G | D | | G |

And I was born in the back seat of a   Greyhound bus   rollin' down Highway Forty-One.

REPEAT CHORUS

VERSE 2

| G | C | G | | | C | | D |

I'm on my way to New Orleans this mornin' and leavin' out of Nashville, Tennessee.

| C | G | | Em | C | G | D | | G |

They're always havin' a good time down on the bayou, Lord. Them delta women think the world of me.

REPEAT CHORUS

OUTRO (REPEAT AND FADE)

| G | F | C | G |

Lord, I was born a ramblin' man.

Guitar Chord Songbooks

Each 6" x 9" book includes complete lyrics, chord symbols, and guitar chord diagrams.

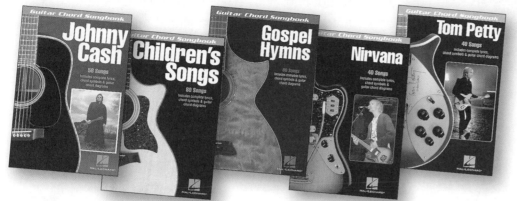

Acoustic Hits
00701787 . . . . $14.99

Acoustic Rock
00699540 . . . . $22.99

Alabama
00699914 . . . . $14.95

The Beach Boys
00699566 . . . . $19.99

Bluegrass
00702585 . . . . $14.99

Johnny Cash
00699648 . . . . $19.99

Children's Songs
00699539 . . . . $17.99

Christmas Carols
00699536 . . . . $14.99

Christmas Songs
00119911 . . . . $14.99

Eric Clapton
00699567 . . . . $19.99

Classic Rock
00699598 . . . . $20.99

Coffeehouse Hits
00703318 . . . . $14.99

Country
00699534 . . . . $17.99

Country Favorites
00700609 . . . . $14.99

Country Hits
00140859 . . . . $14.99

Country Standards
00700608 . . . . $12.95

Cowboy Songs
00699636 . . . . $19.99

Creedence Clearwater Revival
00701786 . . . . $16.99

Jim Croce
00148087 . . . . $14.99

Crosby, Stills & Nash
00701609 . . . . $17.99

John Denver
02501697 . . . . $19.99

Neil Diamond
00700606 . . . . $22.99

Disney – 2nd Edition
00295786 . . . . $19.99

The Doors
00699888 . . . . $22.99

Eagles
00122917 . . . . $19.99

Early Rock
00699916 . . . . $14.99

Folksongs
00699541 . . . . $16.99

Folk Pop Rock
00699651 . . . . $17.99

40 Easy Strumming Songs
00115972 . . . . $16.99

Four Chord Songs
00701611 . . . . $16.99

Glee
00702501 . . . . $14.99

Gospel Hymns
00700463 . . . . $16.99

Grateful Dead
00139461 . . . . $17.99

Green Day
00103074 . . . . $17.99

Irish Songs
00701044 . . . . $16.99

Michael Jackson
00137847 . . . . $14.99

Billy Joel
00699632 . . . . $22.99

Elton John
00699732 . . . . $17.99

Ray LaMontagne
00130337 . . . . $12.99

Latin Songs
00700973 . . . . $14.99

Love Songs
00701043 . . . . $14.99

Bob Marley
00701704 . . . . $17.99

Bruno Mars
00125332 . . . . $12.99

Paul McCartney
00385035 . . . . $19.99

Steve Miller
00701146 . . . . $12.99

Modern Worship
00701801 . . . . $19.99

Motown
00699734 . . . . $19.99

Willie Nelson
00148273 . . . . $17.99

Nirvana
00699762 . . . . $17.99

Roy Orbison
00699752 . . . . $19.99

Peter, Paul & Mary
00103013 . . . . $19.99

Tom Petty
00699883 . . . . $17.99

Pink Floyd
00139116 . . . . $17.99

Pop/Rock
00699538 . . . . $19.99

Praise & Worship
00699634 . . . . $14.99

Elvis Presley
00699633 . . . . $17.99

Queen
00702395 . . . . $17.99

Red Hot Chili Peppers
00699710 . . . . $24.99

The Rolling Stones
00137716 . . . . $19.99

Bob Seger
00701147 . . . . $16.99

Carly Simon
00121011 . . . . $14.99

Sting
00699921 . . . . $24.99

Three Chord Acoustic Songs
00123860 . . . . $16.99

Three Chord Songs
00699720 . . . . $17.99

Two-Chord Songs
00119236 . . . . $16.99

U2
00137744 . . . . $19.99

Hank Williams
00700607 . . . . $16.99

Stevie Wonder
00120862 . . . . $14.99

Prices and availability subject to change without notice.

HAL•LEONARD®
Visit Hal Leonard online at **www.halleonard.com**

The Strum & Sing series for guitar and ukulele provides an unplugged and pared-down approach to your favorite songs – just the chords and the lyrics, with nothing fancy. These easy-to-play arrangements are designed for both aspiring and professional musicians.

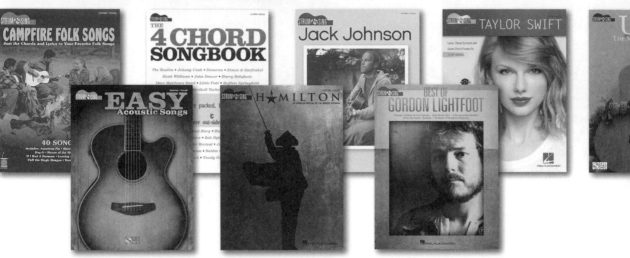

GUITAR

Acoustic Classics
00191891 ....$15.99

Adele
00159855 ....$12.99

Sara Bareilles
00102354 ....$12.99

The Beatles
00172234 ....$17.99

Blues
00159335 ....$12.99

Zac Brown Band
02501620 ....$19.99

Colbie Caillat
02501725 ....$14.99

Campfire Folk Songs
02500686 ....$15.99

Chart Hits of 2014-2015
00142554 ....$12.99

Chart Hits of 2015-2016
00156248 ....$12.99

Best of Kenny Chesney
00142457 ....$14.99

Christmas Carols
00348351 ....$14.99

Christmas Songs
00171332 ....$14.99

Kelly Clarkson
00146384 ....$14.99

Coffeehouse Songs for Guitar
00285991 ....$14.99

Leonard Cohen
00265489 ....$14.99

Dear Evan Hansen
00295108 ....$16.99

John Denver Collection
02500632 ....$17.99

Disney
00233900 ....$17.99

Eagles
00157994 ....$14.99

Easy Acoustic Songs
00125478 ....$19.99

Billie Eilish
00363094 ....$14.99

The Five-Chord Songbook
02501718 ....$14.99

Folk Rock Favorites
02501669 ....$14.99

Folk Songs
02501482 ....$14.99

The Four-Chord Country Songbook
00114936 ....$15.99

The Four Chord Songbook
02501533 ....$14.99

Four Chord Songs
00249581 ....$16.99

The Greatest Showman
00278383 ....$14.99

Hamilton
00217116 ....$15.99

Jack Johnson
02500858 ....$19.99

Robert Johnson
00191890 ....$12.99

Carole King
00115243 ....$10.99

Best of Gordon Lightfoot
00139393 ....$15.99

Dave Matthews Band
02501078 ....$10.95

John Mayer
02501636 ....$19.99

The Most Requested Songs
02501748 ....$16.99

Jason Mraz
02501452 ....$14.99

**Tom Petty –
Wildflowers & All the Rest**
00362682 ....$14.99

Elvis Presley
00198890 ....$12.99

Queen
00218578 ....$12.99

Rock Around the Clock
00103625 ....$12.99

Rock Ballads
02500872 ....$9.95

Rocketman
00300469 ....$17.99

Ed Sheeran
00152016 ....$14.99

The Six-Chord Songbook
02502277 ....$17.99

Chris Stapleton
00362625 ....$19.99

Cat Stevens
00116827 ....$17.99

Taylor Swift
00159856 ....$14.99

The Three-Chord Songbook
00211634 ....$12.99

Top Christian Hits
00156331 ....$12.99

Top Hits of 2016
00194288 ....$12.99

Keith Urban
00118558 ....$14.99

The Who
00103667 ....$12.99

Yesterday
00301629 ....$14.99

Neil Young – Greatest Hits
00138270 ....$15.99

UKULELE

The Beatles
00233899 ....$16.99

Colbie Caillat
02501731 ....$10.99

Coffeehouse Songs
00138238 ....$14.99

John Denver
02501694 ....$17.99

The 4-Chord Ukulele Songbook
00114331 ....$16.99

Jack Johnson
02501702 ....$19.99

John Mayer
02501706 ....$10.99

The Most Requested Songs
02501453 ....$15.99

Jason Mraz
02501753 ....$14.99

Pop Songs for Kids
00284415 ....$16.99

Sing-Along Songs
02501710 ....$16.99

HAL•LEONARD®

halleonard.com
Visit our website to see full song lists
or order from your favorite retailer.

*Prices, contents and availability
subject to change without notice.*

easy GUITAR play along

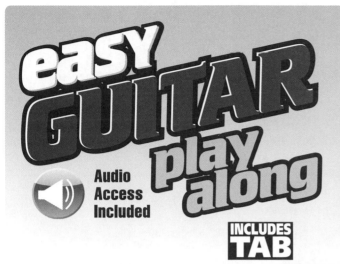

Audio Access Included

INCLUDES TAB

The *Easy Guitar Play Along®* series features streamlined transcriptions of your favorite songs. Just follow the tab, listen to the audio to hear how the guitar should sound, and then play along using the backing tracks. Playback tools are provided for slowing down the tempo without changing pitch and looping challenging parts. The melody and lyrics are included in the book so that you can sing or simply follow along.

1. ROCK CLASSICS
Jailbreak • Living After Midnight • Mississippi Queen • Rocks Off • Runnin' Down a Dream • Smoke on the Water • Strutter • Up Around the Bend.
00702560 Book/CD Pack....... $14.99

2. ACOUSTIC TOP HITS
About a Girl • I'm Yours • The Lazy Song • The Scientist • 21 Guns • Upside Down • What I Got • Wonderwall.
00702569 Book/CD Pack....... $14.99

3. ROCK HITS
All the Small Things • Best of You • Brain Stew (The Godzilla Remix) • Californication • Island in the Sun • Plush • Smells Like Teen Spirit • Use Somebody.
00702570 Book/CD Pack....... $14.99

4. ROCK 'N' ROLL
Blue Suede Shoes • I Get Around • I'm a Believer • Jailhouse Rock • Oh, Pretty Woman • Peggy Sue • Runaway • Wake Up Little Susie.
00702572 Book/CD Pack....... $14.99

6. CHRISTMAS SONGS
Have Yourself a Merry Little Christmas • A Holly Jolly Christmas • The Little Drummer Boy • Run Rudolph Run • Santa Claus Is Comin' to Town • Silver and Gold • Sleigh Ride • Winter Wonderland.
00101879 Book/CD Pack......... $14.99

7. BLUES SONGS FOR BEGINNERS
Come On (Part 1) • Double Trouble • Gangster of Love • I'm Ready • Let Me Love You Baby • Mary Had a Little Lamb • San-Ho-Zay • T-Bone Shuffle.
00103235 Book/
   Online Audio..........$17.99

9. ROCK SONGS FOR BEGINNERS
Are You Gonna Be My Girl • Buddy Holly • Everybody Hurts • In Bloom • Otherside • The Rock Show • Santa Monica • When I Come Around.
00103255 Book/CD Pack.....$14.99

10. GREEN DAY
Basket Case • Boulevard of Broken Dreams • Good Riddance (Time of Your Life) • Holiday • Longview • 21 Guns • Wake Me up When September Ends • When I Come Around.
00122322 Book/
   Online Audio........$16.99

11. NIRVANA
All Apologies • Come As You Are • Heart Shaped Box • Lake of Fire • Lithium • The Man Who Sold the World • Rape Me • Smells Like Teen Spirit.
00122325 Book/
   Online Audio........ $17.99

13. AC/DC
Back in Black • Dirty Deeds Done Dirt Cheap • For Those About to Rock (We Salute You) • Hells Bells • Highway to Hell • Rock and Roll Ain't Noise Pollution • T.N.T. • You Shook Me All Night Long.
14042895 Book/
   Online Audio........ $17.99

14. JIMI HENDRIX – SMASH HITS
All Along the Watchtower • Can You See Me • Crosstown Traffic • Fire • Foxey Lady • Hey Joe • Manic Depression • Purple Haze • Red House • Remember • Stone Free • The Wind Cries Mary.
00130591 Book/
   Online Audio........$24.99

HAL•LEONARD®
www.halleonard.com

Prices, contents, and availability subject to change without notice.

EASY GUITAR WITH NOTES & TAB

This series features simplified arrangements with notes, tab, chord charts, and strum and pick patterns.

MIXED FOLIOS

00702287 Acoustic $19.99	00196954 Contemporary Disney $19.99	00702268 1990s Rock $24.99
00702002 Acoustic Rock Hits for Easy Guitar $15.99	00702239 Country Classics for Easy Guitar..............$24.99	00369043 Rock Songs for Kids $14.99
00702166 All-Time Best Guitar Collection $19.99	00702257 Easy Acoustic Guitar Songs $17.99	00109725 Once $14.99
00702232 Best Acoustic Songs for Easy Guitar.........$16.99	00702041 Favorite Hymns for Easy Guitar...............$12.99	00702187 Selections from
00119835 Best Children's Songs..........................$16.99	00222701 Folk Pop Songs..................................$17.99	O Brother Where Art Thou? $19.99
00703055 The Big Book of Nursery Rhymes	00126894 Frozen $14.99	00702178 100 Songs for Kids $16.99
& Children's Songs.....................$16.99	00333922 Frozen 2 ....$14.99	00702515 Pirates of the Caribbean $17.99
00698978 Big Christmas Collection.......................$19.99	00702286 Glee $16.99	00702125 Praise and Worship for Guitar $14.99
00702394 Bluegrass Songs for Easy Guitar $15.99	00702160 The Great American Country Songbook...$19.99	00287930 Songs from *A Star Is Born, The Greatest*
00289632 Bohemian Rhapsody............................$19.99	00702148 Great American Gospel for Guitar...........$14.99	*Showman, La La Land*, and More Movie Musicals....$16.99
00703387 Celtic Classics $16.99	00702050 Great Classical Themes for Easy Guitar......$9.99	00702285 Southern Rock Hits.............................$12.99
00224808 Chart Hits of 2016-2017 ....$14.99	00275088 The Greatest Showman $17.99	00156420 Star Wars Music.................................$16.99
00267383 Chart Hits of 2017-2018 ....$14.99	00148030 Halloween Guitar Songs.......................$14.99	00121535 30 Easy Celtic Guitar Solos $16.99
00334293 Chart Hits of 2019-2020 ....$16.99	00702273 Irish Songs.......................................$14.99	00244654 Top Hits of 2017................................$14.99
00403479 Chart Hits of 2021-2022 ....$16.99	00192503 Jazz Classics for Easy Guitar $16.99	00283786 Top Hits of 2018................................$14.99
00702149 Children's Christian Songbook...............$9.99	00702275 Jazz Favorites for Easy Guitar $17.99	00302269 Top Hits of 2019................................$14.99
00702028 Christmas Classics $8.99	00702274 Jazz Standards for Easy Guitar $19.99	00355779 Top Hits of 2020................................$14.99
00101779 Christmas Guitar $14.99	00702162 Jumbo Easy Guitar Songbook $24.99	00374083 Top Hits of 2021................................$16.99
00702141 Classic Rock $8.95	00232285 La La Land $16.99	00702294 Top Worship Hits................................$17.99
00159642 Classical Melodies $12.99	00702258 Legends of Rock $14.99	00702255 VH1's 100 Greatest Hard Rock Songs $34.99
00253933 Disney/Pixar's Coco $16.99	00702189 MTV's 100 Greatest Pop Songs..............$34.99	00702175 VH1's 100 Greatest Songs
00702203 CMT's 100 Greatest Country Songs...........$34.99	00702272 1950s Rock $16.99	of Rock and Roll.........................$34.99
00702283 The Contemporary	00702271 1960s Rock $16.99	00702253 Wicked $12.99
Christian Collection $16.99	00702270 1970s Rock $24.99	
	00702269 1980s Rock $16.99	

ARTIST COLLECTIONS

00702267 AC/DC for Easy Guitar...........................$16.99	00702245 Elton John —	00702252 Frank Sinatra — Nothing But the Best $12.99
00156221 Adele – 25 ....$16.99	Greatest Hits 1970–2002 ....$19.99	00702010 Best of Rod Stewart.............................$17.99
00396889 Adele – 30 ....$19.99	00129855 Jack Johnson $17.99	00702049 Best of George Strait............................$17.99
00702040 Best of the Allman Brothers....................$16.99	00702204 Robert Johnson $16.99	00702259 Taylor Swift for Easy Guitar...................$15.99
00702865 J.S. Bach for Easy Guitar........................$15.99	00702234 Selections from Toby Keith —	00359800 Taylor Swift – Easy Guitar Anthology........$24.99
00702169 Best of The Beach Boys.........................$16.99	35 Biggest Hits...........................$12.95	00702260 Taylor Swift — Fearless $14.99
00702292 The Beatles — 1 ....$22.99	00702003 Kiss $16.99	00139727 Taylor Swift — 1989 ....$19.99
00125796 Best of Chuck Berry.............................$16.99	00702216 Lynyrd Skynyrd $17.99	00115960 Taylor Swift — Red $16.99
00702201 The Essential Black Sabbath $15.99	00702182 The Essential Bob Marley $16.99	00253667 Taylor Swift — Reputation $17.99
00702250 blink-182 — Greatest Hits $17.99	00146081 Maroon 5..$14.99	00702290 Taylor Swift — Speak Now $16.99
02501615 Zac Brown Band — The Foundation $17.99	00121925 Bruno Mars – Unorthodox Jukebox $12.99	00232849 Chris Tomlin Collection – 2nd Edition.....$14.99
02501621 Zac Brown Band —	00702248 Paul McCartney — All the Best $14.99	00702226 Chris Tomlin — See the Morning...........$12.95
You Get What You Give $16.99	00125484 The Best of MercyMe...........................$12.99	00148643 Train..$14.99
00702043 Best of Johnny Cash.............................$17.99	00702209 Steve Miller Band —	00702427 U2 — 18 Singles $19.99
00702090 Eric Clapton's Best...............................$16.99	Young Hearts (Greatest Hits) $12.95	00702108 Best of Stevie Ray Vaughan $17.99
00702086 Eric Clapton —	00124167 Jason Mraz.......................................$15.99	00279005 The Who $14.99
from the Album Unplugged.............$17.99	00702096 Best of Nirvana...................................$16.99	00702123 Best of Hank Williams $15.99
00702202 The Essential Eric Clapton $17.99	00702211 The Offspring — Greatest Hits $17.99	00194548 Best of John Williams $14.99
00702053 Best of Patsy Cline...............................$17.99	00138026 One Direction $17.99	00702228 Neil Young — Greatest Hits...................$17.99
00222697 Very Best of Coldplay – 2nd Edition $17.99	00702030 Best of Roy Orbison.............................$17.99	00119133 Neil Young — Harvest..........................$14.99
00702229 The Very Best of	00702144 Best of Ozzy Osbourne.........................$14.99	
Creedence Clearwater Revival.............$16.99	00702279 Tom Petty...$17.99	
00702145 Best of Jim Croce.................................$16.99	00102911 Pink Floyd...$17.99	
00702278 Crosby, Stills & Nash $12.99	00702139 Elvis Country Favorites.........................$19.99	
14042809 Bob Dylan...$15.99	00702293 The Very Best of Prince.........................$19.99	
00702276 Fleetwood Mac —	00699415 Best of Queen for Guitar $16.99	Prices, contents and availability
Easy Guitar Collection.................$17.99	00109279 Best of R.E.M......................................$14.99	subject to change without notice.
00139462 The Very Best of Grateful Dead $16.99	00702208 Red Hot Chili Peppers — Greatest Hits...$17.99	
00702136 Best of Merle Haggard.........................$16.99	00198960 The Rolling Stones...............................$17.99	
00702227 Jimi Hendrix — Smash Hits $19.99	00174793 The Very Best of Santana......................$16.99	
00702288 Best of Hillsong United $12.99	00702196 Best of Bob Seger...............................$16.99	
00702236 Best of Antonio Carlos Jobim.................$15.99	00146046 Ed Sheeran $17.99	

HAL•LEONARD®

Visit Hal Leonard online at **halleonard.com**